# MANAGEMENT EXCELLENCE
# THROUGH QUALITY

# MANAGEMENT EXCELLENCE THROUGH QUALITY

## Thomas J. Barry

**ASQC Quality Press**
Milwaukee, Wisconsin

# MANAGEMENT EXCELLENCE THROUGH QUALITY

Thomas J. Barry

Library of Congress Cataloging-in-Publication Data

Barry, Thomas J.
   Management excellence through quality / Thomas J. Barry.
      p.  cm.
   Includes bibliographical references and index.
   ISBN 0-87389-117-1
   1. Total quality management.   I. Title.
HD62.15.B37   1991
658.5'62 — dc20                                                       91-3350
                                                                        CIP

10 9 8 7 6 5 4 3 2 1

ISBN 0-87389-117-1

*Acquisitions Editor: Jeanine L. Lau*
*Production Editor: Mary Beth Nilles*
*Set in Cheltenham by DanTon Typographers. Cover design by Wayne Dober. Printed and*
*bound by BookCrafters*

For a free copy of the ASQC Quality Press Publications Catalog, including
ASQC membership information, call 800-952-6587.

Printed in the United States of America

ASQC Quality Press
611 East Wisconsin Avenue
Milwaukee, Wisconsin 53202

*In dedication to my special friend, Kuan, and the Loo family*

# Contents

# Introduction

Excellence is the practical manifestation of quality. The journey to management excellence is achieved by a strategic plan to implement Total Quality Management (TQM) in the entire organization. It is a systematic, strategic process for organizational excellence.

TQM is not a fad. It is a natural evolution of all the effective management techniques that are currently being applied by excellent organizations. It is a practical approach for excellence deployment.

TQM is a journey, not a destination. It requires total management commitment to use practical techniques that fit the current organizational culture. This book is not a book of theories but one of practical techniques that will assist management in the public and private sectors during this journey.

Chapter 6, "Taking Ownership for TQM," is a road map that can be followed in white collar environments to achieve management excellence.

# CHAPTER 1

# MANAGEMENT EXCELLENCE

Management excellence is not a God-given right of any organization. It is achieved by a strategic approach to management within the organization.

During our management careers, we have all been exposed to various recommendations and techniques to achieve management excellence. However, many of the approaches and techniques do not work as effectively as they were communicated, so we continue our search for the Holy Grail.

We have overlooked the fact that different management approaches work in some organizations while having a negative impact in others.

We must develop an organizational focus of Total Quality Management (TQM). This focus will not be a program with a start and an end; rather, it is a strategic deployment plan that will not end. It will focus on constant quality improvement within the entire organization.

TQM is a management technique whose time has come. It has been demonstrated around the world as a technique that works in white collar environments, both in the public and private sectors. It is an approach that requires top management involvement and commitment. It cannot be delegated to the quality coordinator or director of quality. The CEO, agency head, prime minister, dean,

1

or president must take personal responsibility for a strategic approach to excellence.

People in organizations watch the behavior of the individual sitting in the corner office. It is by this person's behavior that the organization starts on the journey toward management excellence.

TQM creates an environment that produces excellence. It is an approach that can modify or completely change the organizational culture. However, changing an organizational culture may take years, because you are attempting to change people's attitudes.

# Organizational culture

Before starting this journey toward excellence, we must examine the current organizational culture:

- A set of beliefs
- Values
- Attitudes
- Philosophies of the human environment
- A set of common habits

## A set of beliefs

What are the specific beliefs, such as respect for the individual, on which the organization is based?

## Values

What are the values, like the value of a customer to the organization, that the organization has established within its culture?

## Attitudes

What are employees' attitudes toward having their personal reputation tied to the organization?

## Philosophies of the human environment

What philosophy has management adopted toward managing the human resource within the organization?

## A set of common habits

What are the common habits within the organization, like taking ownership for individual work output and signing your name to the product?

# Cultures within organizations

Various cultures also exist at macro and micro levels within organizations. Take, for example, the Department of Defense. At the Pentagon, a unique culture has been established over many years of tradition that can be tied to the five characteristics identified earlier.

Within the Pentagon we discover that each branch of the armed forces has its own culture developed over many years. Within organizations like the U.S. Navy, we discover additional unique cultures as we flow down the organization. All branches of the armed forces have unique cultures, and within their unique macro-cultures we find micro-cultures.

The Navy's overall culture can be clearly defined. As you look within its overall organization, you will discover that individual organizations like the Naval Research Laboratories and naval bases have developed a micro-culture within the overall culture of the Navy. This micro-culture can be broken down to working units in the range of 300–500 employees.

Most executives can clearly define the preceding five characteristics for their organization and fully communicate its unique culture. The question is, can the first-line manager and the average employee also describe the culture?

If the average employee has no idea what the organization's culture is, then, all we have is an executive culture.

If the current organizational culture has not been clearly defined and communicated within the entire organization, then doing so is the first step prior to the implementation of a TQM approach. First, we must determine the existing organizational culture, and then we may determine how a TQM approach will fit it.

TQM advocates the development of: true "customer orientation," teamwork, and inter-unit cooperation; structured problem-solving; a reliance on Quality Assurance (QA); standards and measurement; a system of rewards and recognition for excellence; and senior management's long-term commitment to the ongoing process of improving quality.

TQM stresses achievement of no defects, no bad practices, and no unsatisfied customers. It also creates a working environment that will contribute to positive morale—workers' attitude toward the organization's goals and objectives. TQM will nurture the organizational culture to produce a working environment in which people willingly take ownership for their work. TQM is a systematic, strategic process with a practical approach to achieving organizational excellence.

## TOTAL QUALITY MANAGEMENT

| IS: | IS NOT: |
|---|---|
| A systematic way to improve products and services | A new program |
| A structured approach to identifying and solving problems | "Fighting fires" |
| Long-term | Short-term |
| Conveyed by management actions | Conveyed by slogans |
| Supported by statistical quality control | Driven by statistical quality control |
| Practiced by everyone | Delegated to subordinates |

**Table 1.1**

The principle elements of TQM are straightforward and embrace a common-sense approach to management. However, each of the individual elements must be integrated into a structured whole to succeed. TQM is a strategic approach with elements that require strategic planning and excellence deployment. Here is an overview of its principles:

- A focus on the customer
- A long-term commitment
- Top management support and direction
- Employee involvement
- Effective and renewed communications
- Reliance on standards and measures
- Commitment to training
- Rewards and recognition
- Quality assurance

## A focus on the customer

Every department and work unit has a customer, whether it be internal or external. TQM advocates that managers and employees become so customer-focused that they continually find new ways to meet or exceed customers' expectations, thus creating not only customer satisfaction but also customer loyalty.

# A long-term commitment

Public and private sector experience in the U.S. and abroad shows that substantial gains come only after management makes a long-term commitment—usually five years or more. However, in a majority of organizations, positive results come within the first year.

# Top management support and direction

Top management must be the driving force behind TQM. Senior managers must exhibit personal support by using Quality Improvement (QI) concepts in their management style, incorporating quality in their strategic planning process, and providing financial and staff support.

# Employee involvement

Full employee participation and empowerment is also an integral part of the process. Each employee must be a partner in achieving quality goals. Teamwork involves managers, supervisors, and employees in improving service delivery, solving systemic problems, and correcting errors in all parts of work processes.

# Effective and renewed communications

The power of internal communication, both vertical and horizontal, is central to employee involvement. Regular and meaningful communication at all levels must occur. This will allow an organization to adjust its ways of operating and reinforce the commitment to TQM at the same time.

# Reliance on standards and measures

Measurement is the springboard to involvement, allowing the organization to initiate corrective action, set priorities, and evaluate progress. Standards and measures should reflect customer requirements and expectations.

# Commitment to training

Training is absolutely vital to the success of TQM. The process usually begins with awareness training for teams of top-level managers. This is followed by teams of mid-level managers, and finally by nonmanagers. Next comes identification of areas of concentration or of functional areas where TQM will first be introduced. Implementing TQM requires additional skill training, which is also conducted in teams.

# Rewards and recognition

All organizations have various means of recognizing correct behavior. Keep in mind that when behavior is rewarded, it will be repeated. The reward can come in many different methods, from individual to group. However, under TQM, it appears that team and group rewards produce greater results.

# Quality assurance

A management system must be in place to support a systematic, strategic process for excellence. Quality assurance (QA) is a validation process to ensure measurement accuracy and standardization. The QA system focuses on constant incremental quality improvement measurements and results. It is a system designed to assist management in the journey toward excellence, not another organizational control.

TQM asks managers to accept ownership for the environment of their organizations and to create an excellence culture. Managers must realize that in many cases, TQM will require a substantial shift in management approaches and a cultural change. However, if used effectively, TQM can eliminate deeply rooted negative cultural perceptions.

TQM eliminates the finger-pointing that normally accompanies a problem and often keeps the causes of the problem from being understood. Instead, TQM requires that someone take ownership for the problem and resolve it.

TQM means working collectively to resolve problems in an environment of mutual responsibility. TQM emphasizes that problems are systemic in nature; therefore, they are not necessarily the fault of the individual worker but rather of the way a process is structured.

At its simplest, TQM provides a strategic deployment method for identifying problems, assessing needed corrective actions, and taking those actions, all without laying blame. TQM stresses achievement of no defects, no bad practices, and no unsatisfied customers. Success or failure is a collective responsibility.

From the most senior level down, managers need to drive the process and incorporate the philosophy of TQM into their management styles. Since TQM focuses on management's responsibility to resolve systemic problems, managers must be prepared for an environment of change.

Management excellence is realized when the organization has established a quality culture that is clearly understood at every level. Any individual in the organization can be proud to be identified with such an environment.

## CHARACTERISTICS OF A QUALITY CULTURE

| IS: | IS NOT: |
| --- | --- |
| Listening to customers to learn their requirements | Assuming you know what customers require |
| Identifying the cost of quality | Overlooking the hidden costs of poor quality |
| "Doing the right thing right the first time" | Doing it over to make it right |
| A continuous improvement process | A one-time "fix" |
| Taking ownership at all organizational levels | Assigning responsibility for quality to one department |
| Demonstrating executive leadership | Delegating responsibility for quality |

**Table 1.2**

# Total commitment needed

TQM requires total commitment, participation, and recognition at all levels of an organization to achieve management excellence. Research has found that substantial support of TQM at the top management level is absolutely essential. Likewise, real commitment from first-line managers and employees is critical.

Obtaining support for a TQM approach from first-line managers and employees is not as difficult as it would seem. It occurs as people in the organization realize that this approach makes their daily work responsibilities easier to accomplish.

Middle managers, in spite of what some people say, will also embrace TQM. Middle managers are survivors, and in many organizations they are the key to management excellence. They understand the organization more than any other level of management does and will fully support TQM if they are involved from day one in developing the organizational strategy and implementation.

Middle managers will embrace TQM if they are shown that it will make their role easier. I think we can safely say that few middle managers enjoy managing with leaner resources. However, in today's organizations, you are going to have leaner resources to get the job done. Investing in the education of middle managers will help them understand how this will help and not hurt.

When we look inside the typical pyramid organization at some of the functions of the three key levels of management, the principles of TQM fit them all (see Fig. 1.1).

**Figure 1.1:   Functions of management**

Middle managers are the key to making the organization's strategic plan a reality. Because of this, and the fact that TQM is a strategic focus, we realize how important it is to gain their support. They are facing the major challenge: resources are being reduced while more is being requested.

The TQM approach will make complete sense to middle managers, since they are searching for a method to help them continue to be survivors. If they do not support TQM, they should be requested to come up with a more effective approach to managing the organization with limited resources.

TQM is here to stay. It is the only effective way to manage a complex organization with limited resources. Middle managers will embrace TQM if the knowledge they are given makes sense and they see it tied directly to their role as middle managers.

TQM is a practical strategic management approach to achieving excellence in an organization. However, to achieve excellence within an organization, we must focus on four key areas (see Fig. 1.2).

The model is dynamic and is in constant motion. It is divided into four equal parts, and the focus of attention should start with leadership/management and end at process focus. The rotation would be like the hour hand of a clock starting at 12 and moving through each of the four parts on its journey toward excellence.

# Leadership is key

We must first have leadership and management for quality improvement. Next, the leaders and managers must create an organizational structure that will support a continuous quality improvement strategy. Once the right organization is in place, we can then create a motivational environment to increase quality and

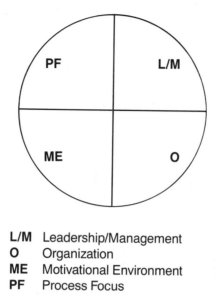

**L/M** Leadership/Management
**O** Organization
**ME** Motivational Environment
**PF** Process Focus

**Figure 1.2:   White collar "quality"/productivity model**

productivity. The last step would be using process focus to increase effectiveness, efficiency, and adaptability. The process focus should also include value analysis techniques that teach people how to do the right thing right the first time and every time.

The key factor in the model will be leadership. Leadership will be the driving force behind an excellence strategy. Leaders play the key role in implementing excellence deployment.

A classic discussion between practitioners and theorists in management concerns the difference between a manager and a leader. I feel the difference is that you work for a manager, while you follow a leader. In today's organizations we are over-managed and under-led.

## Characteristics of leaders

Leaders are visionaries; they have a vision and communicate it to the people within the organization. They are also innovators, since they can make their new ideas happen through people in the organization.

Leaders understand that their internal and external organizational customers are people. They fully understand that the key to quality in any organization is its people. When the people within the organization adopt a quality attitude with individual ownership and commitment, the organization will achieve quality.

I fully agree that some gifted individuals are born with characteristics that help them become leaders. Charisma is a good example. However, leadership is learnable in most organizations. It is a matter of commitment on the part of the individual to understand the requirements of each individual and group within the organization.

The understanding comes in first identifying the requirements. It also includes negotiating with the individual or group to determine if an agreed-upon set of requirements can be reached. When the leader meets the requirements, we have achieved quality. The achievement of the requirements will enhance the leader's role and reputation in the eyes of the people in the organization.

When we think back in our careers as to whom we would identify as a leader, we are using our set of individual requirements. If you think back to all the individuals you identify as leaders, you will suddenly realize that you are recalling behavioral characteristics.

When you identify leaders, you start recalling simple behavioral characteristics. Were the leaders supportive? Did they understand your position or requirements? Did they instill a desire in you to perform at your peak capacity? How did they accomplish this motivational environment?

I think you will begin to understand that we remember leaders by simple behavioral characteristics. This is the key. It is not a laundry list of specific techniques that separate a manager from a leader.

Leaders understand people's requirements in a specific organization and focus on achieving those requirements. If the requirements cannot be met, then they renegotiate them. This renegotiating even includes reorganization so the leader can better satisfy both the internal and external organizational customer.

Leaders make changes within organizations to satisfy their external customer while meeting the requirements of the internal organization.

This is the key to leadership. It is a balancing act. It is not easy to satisfy internal organizational requirements while satisfying the external customer. That is why we have difficulty identifying true leaders today.

We have no difficulty identifying managers. However, to identify leaders is a much more difficult task. It becomes a little easier when we use generic quality knowledge and look at what leaders do when dealing with people.

I believe the future of quality within any organization will be determined directly by that organization's leaders, not by its managers. I am not saying that the managers will not play a key role. What I am saying is that leadership will determine whether the organization solves its quality/productivity focus.

Leaders will look at internal and external customer requirements. They will get the motivational environment started. They must take ownership and show by action, not words, that the organization is committed to achieving quality/productivity.

## People managers

I have concluded that the future of quality/productivity is now in the hands of the people managers. The people managers are those who are extremely capable in creating a motivational environment. They are also practitioners of quality, not lecturers—a characteristic of leaders.

One of the characteristics of leaders is their people skills. They are extremely effective in managing the human resource of an organization and have been identified as people managers. The following are characteristics of effective leaders.

- Leaders work effectively with people.
- Leaders maintain respect.
- Leaders are responsive to the needs and desires of others.
- Leaders are knowledgeable.
- Leaders possess superior motivation.
- Leaders are inspired and enthusiastic.
- Leaders utilize and tap every resource.
- Leaders capitalize on the organizational environment and the leadership of others.

People managers are the key to achieving quality/productivity. They will take the theories of quality and make them happen within their organization.

When you examine the rate of change in today's complex organizations, you realize that the difference between success and failure will be determined by quality through people. The competitiveness of an organization or nation will be determined by its quality/productivity achievements.

Competitiveness is achieved by quality, and quality happens through people. We must stop and realize that the power of a TQM focus will provide excellence.

Organizations must provide leaders with knowledge so they can develop a systematic, strategic process for organizational excellence. Organizations must give them some knowledge of the principles of TQM to affect their attitudes and behavior, and the result will be organizational excellence.

The world and organizations are moving at an extremely rapid pace. We cannot slow down this momentum. We must give the momentum some direction, and that direction can come from a quality focus.

## Leaders make it happen

Nothing happens until you make it happen, and leaders in organizations are those who make it happen. I really feel that it is a simple matter of giving our leaders some basic quality knowledge so that they can rethink their current focus. As their focus changes to quality, it will spread within the organization. It will spread to all levels of management and to employees within the organization.

It is interesting that we do not focus on pride and enthusiasm within organizations. However, leaders understand that without pride and enthusiasm, a quality culture will never be realized. The type of pride required in today's organization is ownership. Ownership occurs when people are willing to sign their work output. We can dictate all types of responsibility in organizations, but we cannot dictate ownership.

Leaders have the ability to get individuals to take pride in their specific output. Leaders create an environment in which individuals feel proud to sign their names to their work output.

This type of environment also contributes to enthusiasm. It is the type of enthusiasm that the leader possesses, and it is contagious. The leader clearly sends out a message of pride and enthusiasm in the organization and its goal and objectives. This message is then relayed to everyone within the organization who comes in contact with the leader.

It is the individual behavior of the leader that will attract others and make them willing to follow. This attraction is what gives the leader the power to get things done within complex organizations without the appearance of a great deal of effort.

The leader willingly accepts this ownership responsibility and creates an environment that contributes directly to pride and enthusiasm. Individual worker pride and enthusiasm must be turned on by someone, and that someone is the leader. In order for an organization to have a quality culture, its leaders must first accept the fact that pride and enthusiasm start with them. When leaders show pride and enthusiasm, the organization will read this signal.

Quality in leadership starts with the leader accepting ownership. This ownership creates an organizational environment that will produce a quality culture. The organizational environment will not change by itself. Exercising leadership comes with the responsibility to accept ownership to make it happen. Quality in leadership means accepting that people within organizations pay attention to what leaders say and do. Leaders must realize that they are different from the average manager. They hold a tremendous amount of power to make a difference. This difference can affect the entire culture of an organization.

Leaders will achieve quality in leadership when they begin to practice their leadership skills with quality. This practice comes in demonstrating that pride, enthusiasm, and ownership for one's output starts at the top.

## Leaders prevent burnout

Leaders can prevent quality burnout. Quality burnout happens when individuals start to lose interest in this new focus on quality. We learned years ago that a Hawthorne effect can occur with a sudden change in performance when a new direction or focus is taken. The lesson learned was to look for long-term results, not a brief change in performance caused by sudden change in leadership direction.

Quality burnout can be prevented when the organization accepts that quality is a journey, not a destination. The journey is a constant, never-ending focus on small incremental improvements. It is not a "foot at a time" but an "inch-by-inch" approach to excellence.

All too often in our managerial careers, we focus on the destination and not the journey. Quality burnout occurs when an organization focuses on a specific destination and not on the journey.

Leaders must also accept the need to develop a model for white collar quality improvement that fits their organization and culture. When leaders accept this fact, they are on their way to solving the white collar quality/productivity issue.

TQM offers a management approach that will work. However, it must be approached in an extremely systematic way.

TQM also means looking at the way organizations function. We organize vertically but function horizontally. TQM forces us to look inside the pyramid at the horizontal organization.

Management excellence through quality is an achievable objective. However, it is not an objective that is achieved and forgotten. It is a journey of constant quality improvement. The journey starts with senior management education and flows down the organization to first-line managers and employees. The ownership for TQM lies with everyone in the organization, but it starts at the top. Once those at the top of the organization start to practice TQM principles, middle-level management will not only support TQM but make it a reality.

# CHAPTER 2

# WHITE-COLLAR
# QUALITY IMPROVEMENT

It is estimated that by the year 2000, the Western world will have approximately 80 percent of its work force in white collar jobs. The push for newer and more sophisticated technologies will continue in the production lines, and more manufacturing concerns will turn to new technologies for increased quality and efficiency.

## Focus on educational excellence

This requires us to focus on white collar effectiveness, efficiency, and adaptability in our organizations. We desperately need a focus on quality education, not only in our business schools but also in our high schools and even our grade schools. I am not recommending that we provide a generation of quality gurus, but we must help our future leaders and managers understand the difference between an absolute efficiency/productivity focus and a quality focus.

It should not be the responsibility of industry and government to educate the white collar worker in quality principles and techniques; it should be the responsibility of our educational system.

This may require a joint venture between the leading quality organizations and local and state educational institutions to transfer knowledge. Many of the leading quality organizations have developed complete training courses that can be shared effectively with educational systems to train the trainer.

We are facing a situation of world leadership and national competitiveness which requires a partnership between our educational system and organizations that have focused on management excellence. The problem is too big even for the federal government.

An organizational focus on white collar quality improvement in the public and private sectors starts with knowledge. However, knowledge of any kind has no effect until it is combined with practice and feedback:

---

### Knowledge + Practice + Feedback = Success
### K + P + F = S

---

All the knowledge in the world in the field of white collar quality will have no impact until it is practiced with feedback. The feedback should indicate if the knowledge has to be modified to fit the organization's culture.

This success is long-term, not short-term. We seem to forget that Japan has taken more than three decades to change the reputation of the quality of its products. The fact that the Japanese still focus on constant quality improvement and provide this knowledge in their educational system gives you an idea of the journey to management excellence.

Success is not easy when you are trying to change people's attitudes. Attitudes are extremely difficult to change since they are part of an organizational culture that has most likely taken years to develop. Attitudes are also difficult to change if our education never communicated how important it is to focus on quality.

The statement that I have made around the world when dealing with white collar quality improvement is:

---

### Quality is 90% attitude and 10% knowledge.

---

The argument that this ratio should be 70/30 or 50/50 or whatever is not the point. The point is that knowledge in the classroom environment is only a small fundamental step. Useful knowledge is power, and it should never stop. We must continue to focus on education in the field of quality and develop feedback systems to determine what needs to be modified.

# Changing attitudes

We must change the attitudes of the work force in industry, schools, hospitals, and governments toward ownership of quality/productivity. We need an attitude that says:

- I take pride in my organization and identify with it.
- I take pride in my work output.
- I know my customers' requirements.
- I will sign my name to my output.
- I really practice "doing the right thing right the first time."

By thinking this way, you take ownership. Suppose you are walking by the phone of someone in your organization, and the phone is ringing without anyone there to pick it up. The question is, would you pick up the phone even though it is not yours and try to help the person who is calling the organization? You take ownership of things when you answer that phone.

Attitude concerns the willingness of employees to indicate their commitment with their behavior.

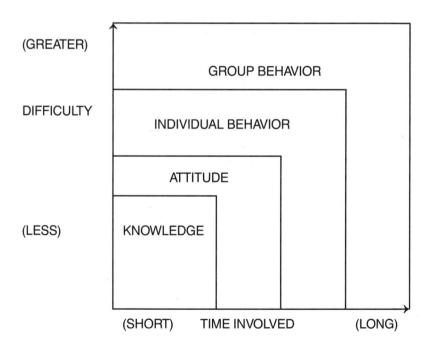

**Figure 2.1:  How to change attitudes and behavior**

We give people knowledge, and this changes their attitudes. They then develop an individual behavior and function as members of organizational groups that display group behavior.

The most difficult and time-consuming task is to change group behavior (see Fig. 2.1). Changing group behavior depends not only on the knowledge we give individuals but also on the current organizational culture.

This is no longer an era in which we can let things happen or watch them happen. We have to make things happen. If we are asking employees to "Do the right thing the first time," we must provide them with the knowledge of the right thing to do and how to do it right the first time.

Knowledge is the beginning of the journey, but the ultimate objective is to create an attitude in the work force that says we are in this together. It makes sense not to have to do work over on Tuesday that was accomplished on Monday.

The argument I hear from managers all over the world is, "But Tom, you don't understand. We don't have the time to do it right the first time." Then I ask, "Don't you find the time to do it over a second time when it was done wrong the first time?" We usually *find* that time, with overtime and use of additional resources.

If this statement makes sense to management, then we must ask why we are allowing it to happen. It is management's responsibility to provide the knowledge to achieve quality/productivity, and it is management's responsibility to begin the journey. This responsibility cannot be delegated.

# A quality focus

White collar environments in both the public and private sectors require a change in our negative attitude toward productivity. We are victims of our education. We were provided with the understanding that productivity means producing more output. That is a negative perception, and it must be changed to focus on quality/productivity.

You can run any organization out of business with a productivity focus. Such a focus is negative, stresses output over input, and encourages all to "work harder, not smarter." In today's organizations we are 100 percent efficient doing rework. Instead, we need a quality focus:

- Effectiveness: customer satisfaction (internal/external)
- Efficiency: productivity the right way
- Adaptability: innovation

When we have a quality focus, first we focus on effectiveness—effectiveness in the eyes of our customer. This focus can be applied in any white collar environment, since all public and private sector organizations have internal/external customers.

Once the customers are identified and their requirements are fully understood, we establish various means of measuring how we maintain and constantly improve customer satisfaction while using the least possible resources. Using the least possible resources efficiently while maintaining effectiveness is productivity the right way.

The next step is adaptability—designing the ability in your process to anticipate changing customer requirements.

A hidden payback of a quality focus is that it also creates an organizational environment that produces high morale. In such a motivational climate, workers voluntarily commit themselves to organizational goals and objectives.

Behavioral scientists and industrial psychologists still don't agree whether there is a direct correlation between positive morale and productivity. However, my practical line and staff management experience for over three decades says there is a direct correlation. When you focus on TQM to achieve management excellence, you create the condition not only of high productivity but also of high quality, which gives you a greater return.

In fact, a total quality focus will produce:

- Effectiveness
- Efficiency
- Adaptability
- Customer satisfaction (internal/external)
- Greater market share
- Greater profit margin
- Morale
- An attitude of "work smarter, not harder"

Productivity cannot be forced in white collar environments. Total quality control is not the answer in white collar environments; Total Quality Management is.

Management at all levels will embrace TQM as an approach to management excellence. An absolute productivity focus like the one we are still teaching in our educational systems will lead any public or private sector organization to absolute failure.

An extremely practical technique that can be used as a flashlight, not a spotlight, is the cost of quality. The cost of quality is broken down into three main areas:

---

### Prevention + Appraisal + Failure = Total Cost of Quality

---

The cost of quality should not be used as a club or a comparison tool between functions within the organization. It is an estimate that should be looked on as a trend in the organization and functional units.

The cost of quality is the cost of avoiding nonconformance and failure. Maintaining quality helps you avoid the compounding costs you would incur from the deviation of not doing the right thing the first time. The concept of "cost of quality" has been brought about to capture top management attention. Individuals at this level have no difficulty understanding the bottom-line impact of focusing on TQM when they see their cost of quality.

For any product or service there are certain costs incurred. The total cost of a product or service must take into consideration the prevention, appraisal, and failure costs related to both labor and materials utilized.

# Costs of nonconformance

Prevention costs are costs associated with preventing nonconformance to requirements. An example is the investment you make in training your employees to do the right job the first time. You do not wait for things to go wrong before correcting them but prevent the wrong things from happening. In other words, you pro-act, not react as is usually the case. Process analysis, defect analysis, and defect prevention are examples of prevention. Rather than exercising control when things go wrong, focus on prevention.

Appraisal costs are costs incurred when you assign the task of inspecting outputs to ensure conformance to requirements. Examples of appraisal tasks are checking, proofreading, auditing, measuring, and reviewing someone else's work output. When you assign someone else to check your work output to ensure it contains no errors, you are doing appraisal. You are incurring extra resources when doing appraisal. If you instill a conscientious attitude to strive to do the right thing the first time, you will not need someone else to check your work output for you.

Failure costs are costs incurred in correcting or reworking outputs that do not conform to requirements. Examples of failure tasks are redoing, reworking, correcting errors, redrawing, scrapping, or fixing outputs that have not conformed to the standards set. Failure results when you have not done the right thing the first time and you end up having to do things over to put them right again. The cumulative effect of not doing the right thing the first time will result in incurring additional costs to correct it.

We must redirect current resources from appraisal into prevention. The payback is a multiplier effect that reduces failure and total cost. Do more prevention tasks than appraisal tasks, and you will automatically bring down your failure cost. By reducing your failure costs, you reduce your total cost of quality.

How soon can you bring down your cost of quality? Again, it depends on the kind of organization you have and its commitment.

The cost of quality in white collar environments can be determined at the lowest level in an organization. A team of employees with its immediate manager can determine where the department's current resources are focused.

The basic approach is to determine where resources are currently focused and redirect them from appraisal to prevention. The cost of quality is not a new accounting system or measurement system. It is an estimate. Its main value is that it gives us a reference point. Its real power comes when we examine the direction of trends and see failure and total costs decrease as prevention increases. The cost of quality:

- is not a financial program

- is not a typical financial measurement
- is not a substitute for the existing accounting system
- is not a program to compare departments, functions or divisions
- is an estimate

The cost of quality is an excellent measure to determine resource allocation within an organization. It will enable management to identify the key areas of current focus and redirect the focus to prevention.

# Achieving customer satisfaction

In white collar environments the most useful measure of quality is customer satisfaction. When we meet the agreed-upon requirements of our customers, we have achieved quality in their eyes. The process of achieving a quality output is to focus constantly on prevention. One way to measure the effect of a quality focus is through the cost of quality, and the standard to look for is "defect-free."

Defect-free does not mean purely zero defects—which many think is impractical or unachievable, especially in a white collar environment—but defect-free in relation to your customer requirements. We should be looking for trends and continuous improvement.

You may be able to satisfy your customer today but not tomorrow. People change, environments change, requirements change. The idea is to be flexible and adaptable enough to meet those challenges. To do that, you should know who your customers are. Understand, negotiate, and agree on the requirements, and focus on prevention.

Once customer satisfaction has been achieved, the next target for improvement is creating customer loyalty. Customer loyalty means that your customer will continue to do business with you even if another organization comes along with a lower price or better terms and conditions.

Customer expectations include:

- Anticipation
- Previous experience
- Competitive comparisons
- Value for money factors
- Advertising influence
- Third party information

Fulfilling customer expectations involves:

- Organizational performance
- Attitudes of employees
- Friendliness
- Skills
- Communication ability

We set a level of expectation in the eyes of our customers. By fulfilling the expectations, we achieve a level of customer satisfaction. Our short-term focus is on customer satisfaction:

$$\frac{\text{Measurement of}}{\text{satisfaction}} = \frac{\text{Fulfillment of Expectation}}{\text{Expectation}} = 100\%$$

Our long-term focus aims for customer loyalty:

$$\frac{\text{Measurement of}}{\text{satisfaction}} = \frac{\text{Fulfillment of Expectation}}{\text{Expectation}} = >100\%$$

When we are able to go beyond customer satisfaction to customer loyalty, we have achieved a real state of management excellence through quality.

Customer loyalty will mean survival for any white collar organization, since the internal/external customer will decide if the organization should survive.

## Practical approach to prevention

A practical application of prevention is, "Do the right thing right the first time." You instill this awareness and consciousness at all times. You cannot afford to do things over a second or third time.

You attempt to think things through before actually performing your work. Often, we are anxious to complete our tasks and do not think about using minimum possible effort or cost. We do not think of consequences or alternatives, nor do we stop to think if the work is really necessary in the first place.

We think we know what the other person wants or means and we try to figure out as best we can, only to find out afterwards that we have not understood that person's requirements, nor are we able to satisfy ourselves or our customers.

Before you embark on that piece of work, make sure you have agreed with your customer on the output required. Make sure your supplier understands your requirements too. There will be times when you suddenly have many things to do at the same time. Check, negotiate, and agree with your customers on their priority.

Your customers are the most important people. Without them, you are not in business. You have no value added to your organization.

White collar quality is the most difficult area to work in when it comes to implementing quality and establishing a feedback measurement system that truly measures progress. However, it is currently being implemented in both private and public sector organizations in America.

Organizations that have found successful techniques and approaches must share this knowledge so that we all can benefit from management excellence.

# CHAPTER 3

# DANCE AND GO WITH IT

Many organizations have a key manager or executive who will oppose the implementation of management excellence. In addition, some organizations have departments or agencies with subcultures that are completely unreceptive to a strategic approach to excellence.

The question is, how can you implement a strategy for excellence when a key executive or agency in a position of power practices something else? This is an extremely difficult position to be in, since it presents a major obstacle to achieving organizational excellence. However, change can come from within the organization, starting at an individual, department, or functional level.

The basic issue is one of limited resources. We are going to have to accomplish more with less in the future. A quality focus will accomplish this, and it allows an individual manager to become a change agent within the organization despite the obstacle. We must realize that this is a long-term process. It is impossible to turn around large bureaucratic organizations overnight. A quality improvement strategy is a long-term commitment.

Solving operational day-to-day problems is what managers and executives get paid for. If we did not have operational day-to-day problems, we would not need managers or executives. A quality improvement strategy is a long-term focus to eliminate the root cause of day-to-day problems.

When we focus on a long-term strategy, we must realize that over a period of time the individuals and individual functions who had been obstacles will eventually embrace an excellence focus, since there is no alternative.

# Surviving obstacles

The answer is "dance and go with it." This is not a recommendation to give up. It is a recommendation for survival. It is a way to survive when a major obstacle prevents you from practicing quality.

If an individual, department, or agency in a power position opposes quality, then you must develop a strategy to go with the flow. Going with the flow does not mean you give up. It means you become a change agent within the organization despite the obstacles.

If you really believe in excellence, then it can and will happen. It will be a slow process, and it will be extremely frustrating at times, but you can make a difference.

Making a difference can be dangerous since we all resist change to some extent. Implementing a quality improvement strategy means change in an organization. Change can be perceived as a tremendous threat to an individual. Some of the reasons that people resist change are:

- Perceived threat to stability
- Economic considerations
- Possible inconvenience
- Uncertainty about the unknown
- Perceived threat to social relationships
- Perceived threat to status symbols

# A missionary for excellence

Becoming a change agent is not easy. I like to look at it as becoming a missionary for excellence. The question is, how do you turn around the negative or neutral attitudes of key individuals in power positions? Well, there is no one answer to this obstacle. It requires total commitment on your part if you have made the decision to become the change agent.

It is not easy, by any means. The basic approach is to go slow, and like a drop of water on a stone, you will eventually leave a mark. A total quality improvement focus will not happen in the entire organization until the obstacles change or are removed, and this may take years. In the meantime, you "dance and go with it."

The obstacles to change must be addressed. They are obstacles that can prevent the successful implementation of a TQM approach to excellence. If the obstacles cannot be completely eliminated, then their negative impact should be minimized. To minimize the resistance to change, the following should at minimum be addressed with an action plan:

- Ensure adequate understanding through effective communication.
- Promote acceptance through participative management at all levels of the organization.
- Maintain an environment of continuing improvement and positive change.
- Follow up.

"Dance and go with it" is a strategic approach to implementing quality within an organization that may encounter some barriers in power positions. We have all experienced the type of situation I have been describing. The approach is to get around the obstacle without a direct confrontation.

Organizations are designed to focus on existing problems, and the more successful an organization is, the more difficult it will be to implement change. "There is nothing more vulnerable than entrenched success."

The organizations that have the greatest exposure to failure are the successful organizations. An attitude develops within these organizations that says, "Why change? If it ain't broke, don't fix it." If we look back at corporations and organizations that no longer exist, we find this type of attitude.

## Constant improvement

One of the most difficult things is to convince a successful organization that it must focus on constant quality improvement. It is difficult for an organization that is successful to understand that success is not a God-given right. It must be earned every day, and it must be protected from competition.

The success of the Japanese is due to a total private and public commitment to education and constant improvement.

Western culture must create such a covenant and a real commitment to the education of the entire population. This is the type of change I have been addressing. How many managers, executives, and educators are willing to make this commitment? It all comes back to ideas discussed in chapter 1: we are dealing with attitudes of the people in power. These people say, "If it ain't broke, don't fix it." The knowledge required to change this attitude will take years to deliver, and it must be packaged to hook them.

I cannot overstress that this is a journey and not a destination. We are trained and educated to focus constantly on the destination. Our culture looks for immediate gratification, and it is reactive, not proactive. We must refocus and think of the journey, and the destination will take care of itself.

The refocus will come with a commitment to excellence. I am not saying that the excellent corporations and organizations have not focused on excellence. What I am saying is that excellence must be packaged and communicated to every employee within the organization.

Each and every employee within the organization should understand the organization's culture and its major priorities. I continuously find that executives can communicate the culture and organizational priorities, but these have not been communicated down the pyramid to the average employee.

The entire process of creating an organizational environment that supports a quality focus can take years to establish, and while this process is going on, the missionary is trying to survive. The way to retain one's sanity is to "dance and go with it."

The determination to "dance and go with it" is for winners, not losers. It is a strategy that accepts that change will come eventually, despite the obstacles.

All organizations, whether public or private, are faced with the same challenge: how do you do more with less? A quality focus is the only way to address this challenge now and in the future. I strongly believe as time passes that obstacles to an excellence focus will be removed one by one as organizations go through this revolutionary change.

"Revolutionary" is a powerful word, but this is what will be required in the organizations that currently have an individual, department, or agency resisting an excellence focus. One of the things we teach in a constant quality improvement process is that you must "walk your talk." The saying I prefer is, "Practice what you preach, or what you preach will not get practiced."

My short experience with the federal government was quite an education. I constantly met government executives at the senior executive service level who preached one thing and practiced another. As I work on a consulting basis with the federal government, I find this is also true at various managerial and executive levels.

However, I must add that I have met some highly knowledgeable and dedicated government executives who have now embraced a strategic approach towards excellence. They are the type of executives who have taken ownership for excellence within their organizations and have become the personal change agents. They have also networked with other executives to share their knowledge and experience on a TQM approach to excellence.

Most of my personal time is spent with executive and managerial levels within various governments on a personal referral basis. When an organization contacts me, it is always driven by a top executive who is trying to make a difference. What I find, in contact after contact, is that they have networked their experience and knowledge and selected outside assistance based on a network of other change agents.

What is unique about the federal government is that priorities change at the top level with each new administration and political appointee. Many of our senior executive-level managers have been exposed to various techniques, recommendations, and fads on how to effectively manage their organizations, depending on the direction of the new administration. However, what many government executives have now realized is that a strategic, systematic organizational process to excellence makes sense. They are becoming individual change agents within a system that in many ways is structured with procedures that prevent excellence.

Having spent 28 years at IBM in numerous managerial line and staff positions, both domestic and international, I can state that even in IBM you have to "dance and go with it." IBM is an excellent company, but even it has its share of mistakes in management.

At the end of a pencil you see an eraser. The eraser is our acknowledgement that we make mistakes. If a company as excellent as IBM can make mistakes in its managerial and executive selection process, then what is going on in less-than-excellent companies?

I am not attacking IBM; it has been my home for 28 years. IBM educated me and gave me international exposure that I could never place a price on. However, even IBM has executives and managers who don't practice what they preach. So even in IBM there are times when you have to "dance and go with it."

At any one day within IBM, 18,000 employees spend their working time being educated. It is estimated that IBM spends close to $1 billion on the education of its employees. To put that into perspective, it means IBM spends more on education than the two largest universities in the world.

IBM requires that every one of its approximately 40,000 managers worldwide attends at least 40 hours of management education a year. It also requires that approximately 32 hours of the 40 hours be focused on people management.

Here we have a worldwide, complex organization that fully understands the importance of knowledge. It also understands the power behind a people focus. It is an organization with a structured, scientific methodology for educating all employees at all levels.

IBM has, in my opinion, one of the most well-managed selection processes in the appointment of an individual to become a manager. With this in mind, if IBM has a well-managed selection process to pick an individual to become a manager, what is going on in the public and private sector where this selection process is not in place?

So, the real issue is that many public and private organizations have managers and executives who not only don't understand what excellence is all about but serve as obstacles to the achievement of excellence. Please keep in mind that "excellence is the practical manifestation of quality."

# Resistance to change

Now we are at the real issue. Someone within the organization in a power position may resist change and stop the focus on excellence by their actions.

The question constantly comes up, "How can I practice quality on a journey toward excellence in a negative organizational environment?" The only practical answer I can give is that you be a change agent within the organization. Accept that it will take time to change organizational environments. It is a journey, not a destination.

"Dance and go with it" is nothing more than a personal strategy to survive as a change agent within an organization that is not ready for excellence, even though you are. It starts with believing that you can make a difference, even if the difference is small. The secret to incremental improvement is that when you total the small improvements, they result in a major improvement.

Since the change must come from within the organization, by accepting the role as a change agent, we accept ownership. Implementing an approach to excellence can start at a small working group level and become a model for the entire work unit.

# The change agent

A change agent can initiate the journey by taking ownership and realizing that we do have a large impact on the work product we produce. It starts with simple process analysis of examining the basic steps we perform to deliver a product and whether any of the steps have defects. It continues with defining our internal and external customers, their requirements, and how to meet them.

The change agent realizes that there is no alternative, since an absolute productivity focus will not work. A change agent realizes fully that it has to start somewhere, so they take ownership on a micro level within the organization and use the proven tools of TQM that fit a micro application.

# CHAPTER 4

## PROCESS FOCUS

A prevention technique that has been proven successful in white collar environments is using a process focus. This technique allows us to closely examine a critical issue in all pyramid organizations. Pyramid organizations are organized vertically but function horizontally. The pyramid organizational structure has survived the test of time and is here to stay. However, we must analyze the structure to determine how to achieve effectiveness, efficiency, and adaptability horizontally. Within the pyramid organization, various functions interact with each other and function as a supplier or a customer. An example appears in Figure 4.1.

Each function has its own pyramid within the entire organizational pyramid. However, each function must interact with other internal functions to accomplish its mission. In today's white collar organizations, this horizontal interaction has become key to the survival of the organization. A process focus allows us not only to determine the interaction of various functions but also to look at the real way organizations function.

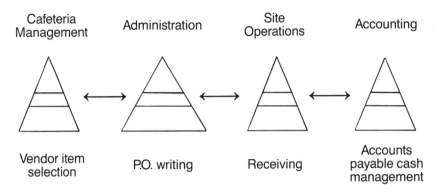

Figure 4.1:   Complex process food services

# A balancing act

This focus is necessary in white collar environments, since we now face a major challenge in our current organizational structures.

The challenge is to balance effectiveness and efficiency. We must look within the organization to determine how the various working units function to benefit the whole.

Sub-optimization is no longer acceptable. We must optimize the effectiveness, efficiency, and adaptability of each working unit to benefit the entire organization. We must look within organizations to determine what individual working units interact with each other to benefit the whole.

To understand and communicate quality measurements, you first have to identify and understand the process or processes you own.

A "process" is the organization of people, procedures, machines, and materials into work activities needed to produce a specified result (work product).

A "process" is also a sequence of activities characterized as having:

- Measurable input(s)
- Value-added activities
- Measurable output(s)
- Repeatability

When we look at the example in Figure 4.1, we start to see how the processes within the organization interact with each other.

Another example is the way a typical organization is structured to deliver a product to its customer (see Fig. 4.2).

Each individual unit has its own mission or function, and within the organization the units interact to accomplish the goals and objectives of the entire organization. If the organization is to realize its goals and objectives, each unit must first look at itself as an individual part of the whole organizational process. Development must look at manufacturing as in internal customer within the organization.

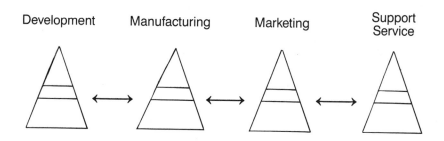

**Figure 4.2:  Complexity of process**

Marketing in turn would look at manufacturing and service support as an internal customer. A "process" focus allows an individual function to step back and examine its suppliers and internal/external customers. It is the most powerful technique available in white collar environments to make the most of the entire organization, not just individual functions within the organization. When we look within our pyramid organizations, we find each individual pyramid interacts with another pyramid in a horizontal position (see Fig. 4.3).

The first step is to determine the major processes that are critical to the organization. We can determine these by starting with the mission statement and working toward the critical processes.

# Mission statement

What is the mission of the organization in the next two years, and what is its strategic outlook?

# Identification of dominant factors of mission

What are the key factors in the mission statement that the organization wants to achieve?

# Establish critical success factors

What are the critical success factors for the organization to achieve its mission?

# Identification of major processes

What are the key processes that drive and support the critical success factors? Who currently owns these processes, and at what level are they functioning?

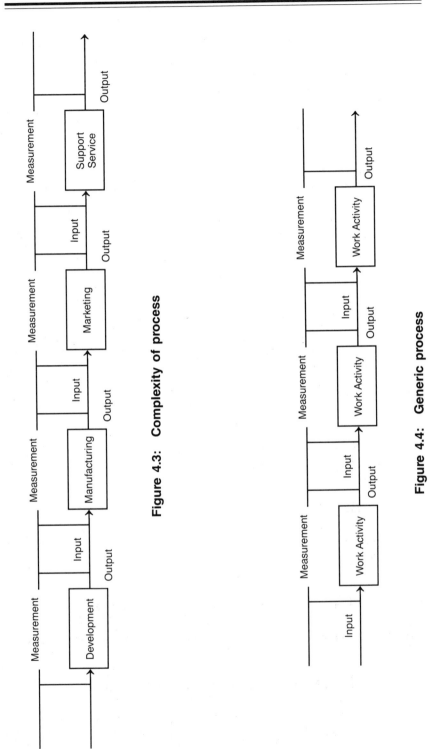

**Figure 4.3: Complexity of process**

**Figure 4.4: Generic process**

# Assess process impact on critical success factors

What is the impact on a critical success factor if a key process does not improve?

# Identification of critical process

Since the mission statement should include an operational and strategic focus on the organizational customer, we can now identify a key customer-driven process.

This is the first step in process analysis. We have now identified a key process, its owner, and their performance level. The next step is to examine what is going on in the current organization (see Fig. 4.4).

Each individual function becomes a supplier or a customer of another function within the organization. Process analysis requires each individual unit to stop and ask some extremely significant questions:

- What other functions interface with the process?
- Have the requirements across other functions been established, understood, and agreed upon?
- Who owns the other functions?
- How can you improve a process outside your immediate ownership?

The major concept of prevention is to remove the defect before it gets to the customer and additional resources have to be invested in doing it over. We must look within the individual process to determine what steps are required to take the input to the output and eliminate non-value-add steps and defects (see Fig. 4.5).

There are four steps to the defect removal cycle. They are:

- Defect identification
- Defect cause analysis
- Development of corrective action
- Testing, evaluating, and implementing

**Step 1:** Having identified the defects, you have to categorize and prioritize them.

**Step 2:** Collect relevant data for cause analysis.

**Step 3:** Once the causes are identified, develop solutions and set new objectives as part of the corrective action plan.

**Step 4:** Having removed the defects, pilot-run the process and evaluate the result before fully implementing the process.

The defect removal cycle is an effective methodology that can prevent a defect from being delivered to a customer. It is a prevention technique that will greatly reduce failure cost, with a resulting decrease in the total cost of quality.

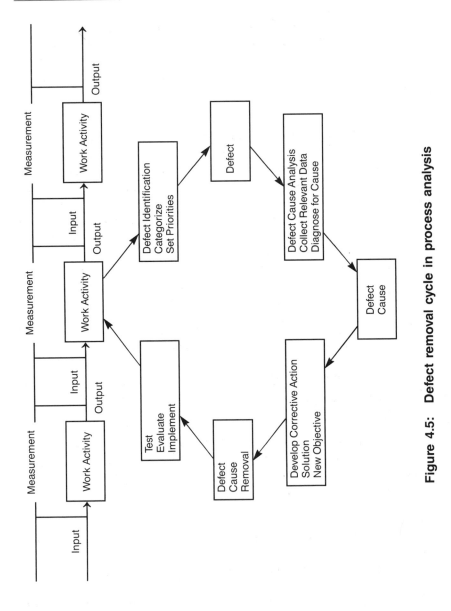

**Figure 4.5: Defect removal cycle in process analysis**

Before removing the defects in the process, ensure that the process is running effectively and efficiently. While an efficient process produces the required output at the lowest possible cost, an effective process produces output that conforms to customer requirements.

There are two ways to do this:

- Establish a measurement mechanism within the process.
- Obtain feedback from your customers.

A customer is one who uses your work output, and a supplier is one who provides you with work input. Customers and suppliers in an organization can be individuals, departments, or functions. Whether you are in finance, marketing, engineering or administration, you have a set of customers and suppliers. You have both internal and external customers and suppliers. Internal customers/suppliers are those within the same department, and external are those outside your department. In a broader sense, you can determine internal customers as those within your organization and external customers as those outside your organization.

Whether they are your internal or external customers, you still have to satisfy their requirements if you are to achieve quality. Satisfying your customer requires you to communicate, understand, negotiate, and agree upon the requirements to be set. Similarly, you will have to do so with your supplier.

The communication process between customers and suppliers generates a motivational atmosphere. A sense of belonging and importance prevails as everyone works toward understanding and satisfying one another's requirements.

Improving the quality of a process is a journey toward defect-free performance. To achieve defect-free status throughout the process is to focus on prevention. Eliminating defects prior to output is prevention. To put the prevention approach into practice is to continuously look out for improvements (see Fig. 4.6).

# Quality defined

Hence we define quality as:

- Conformance to agreed-upon requirements
- Customer/user satisfaction
- Constant evaluation of performance
- Motivational environment

What appears to be missing in many organizations is the correct measurement system. What we are currently measuring is not the true satisfaction level of our customers but our own internal performance. We continuously build additional measurements into our system but fail to include the true measures of our customers' requirements. In fact, my worldwide experience has driven me to conclude that we are worshiping control systems as we are going out of business.

As an example, consider our educational system as a process. Who are the customers? Are they the students, parents, community, government, or industry? How do you measure the level of satisfaction with one or all of them?

The measurement system should provide feedback to indicate if in fact customer satisfaction and perceptions are being satisfied. The measurement system must be driven by the customer, not by the organization's assumption of what the customer needs. Management excellence must be approached in a systematic way. A process focus allows an organization to determine the steps necessary to take an input to an output. More importantly, it forces an organization to focus on its customer and to determine whether the customer is satisfied.

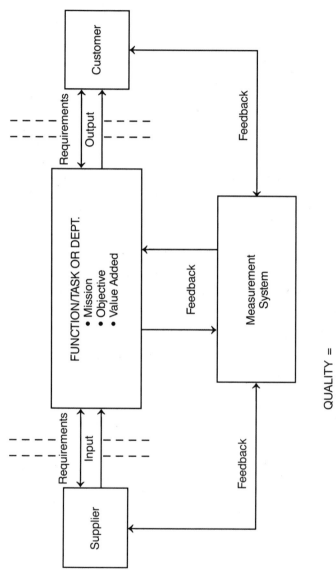

**Figure 4.6: Improving the quality of process**

## TYPICAL REQUIREMENTS OF
## INTERNAL AND EXTERNAL CUSTOMERS

### INTERNAL CUSTOMERS

- Timeliness
- Accuracy
- Clarity
- Thoroughness
- Specification
  Defect rate
  Error rate
  Materials
  Dimension
  Style
  Format
  Sequence
- Physical characteristics
- Completeness

### EXTERNAL CUSTOMERS

- Functionality
- Usability
- Cost/performance
- Reliability
- Availability
- Serviceability
- Marketability
- Installability
- Extendibility

**Table 4.1**

Methods of determining customer requirements include:

- Receipt of your product or service
- Customer surveys and letters
- Sampling procedures and market test
- Customer liaison meetings
- Customer complaints

The argument that you can't measure quality in some white collar environments is not true. You must use a process focus to determine customer requirements and establish a feedback and measurement system that is customer-driven.

The requirements established between the function and the customer should be negotiated so that you may establish standards to measure the satisfaction level. The standard of becoming defect-free in white collar environments is a journey in relation to agreed-upon requirements.

If a function sets a target output of 95 percent of all educational material delivered to its customers within 30 days and the customer accepts the 95 percent standard, then this is the target for defect-free performance. If the material is delivered at the 95 percent level, we have achieved defect-free status in relation to customer requirements.

The object of the function is to focus on constant quality improvement and improve the effectiveness of the 95 percent while accomplishing this level with a minimum of resources.

# Process focus

A process focus is a systematic way of achieving effectiveness and efficiency. The adaptability comes as the function refines the feedback and measurement system. This refinement leads to the ability of a process to modify its output when customer requirements change. The final step in process focus comes when the function can anticipate a change in customer requirements and create customer loyalty.

Another benefit of a process focus is the tie-in of the supplier to the measurement and feedback system. The function is most likely the customer of another process that should negotiate requirements with it. By using a process focus, the function is able to request negotiated input from the supplier to flow it through to the output and satisfy its customer's requirements.

One of the keys to white collar quality improvement comes with a process focus which will produce management excellence leading to effectiveness, efficiency, and adaptability.

When organizations start on this journey and look horizontally, the concept of ownership comes into play. Ownership is holding a specific individual in the vertical organization responsible for the effectiveness, efficiency, and adaptability of a process that functions horizontally.

Ownership requires us to look at the entire process focus from an executive level down to a first-line management level to determine who owns what (see Fig. 4.7).

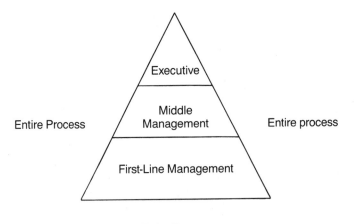

**Figure 4.7: Process management: who owns what**

Ownership can come at various levels of management as a specific process is broken down into sub-process sections. The key is to assign a sub-process owner and then determine how the process is functioning in relationship to effectiveness, efficiency, and adaptability.

The organization should focus on how each individual level of management owns a piece of a major organizational process that in turn affects the entire performance of the major organizational process. Each level of management is responsible for a functioning unit or department that is actually functioning horizontally within the pyramid organization while playing a major role in the entire process (see Fig. 4.8).

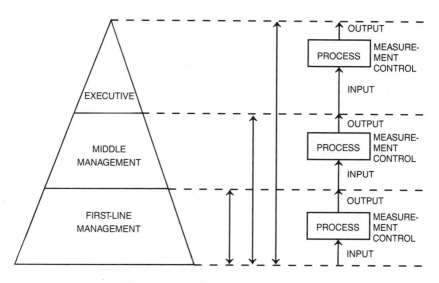

**Figure 4.8:   Process ownership**

A first-line manager in a pyramid organization owns a sub-process of a major organizational process. The first-line manager's sub-process actually functions horizontally while feeding input into the middle manager's process. Middle managers ultimately own their process and the sub-process of all the first-line managers who report to them.

At the executive level, we find complete ownership of the organizational process, since executives are responsible for all levels below them in the pyramid and ultimately own the process.

The process focus forces the issue of who is really responsible for what. It also prevents sub-optimization that might destroy a pyramid organization, since a function could sub-optimize at the cost of the entire organization.

We must focus on solving the entire organization's problems, not the sub-optimization of individual functions. This requires a process focus to achieve management excellence in white collar environments. A process focus starts with the following key questions:

- What other functions interact with the owner's process?
- Have the requirements across other functions been established, understood, and agreed upon?
- Who owns the other functions?

- How can you improve a process outside your immediate ownership?

Having answered the above key questions, we are then in a position to conduct a complete process analysis, which includes the following:

- What are the input needs from supplier?
- What are the customer needs and expectations?
- What are your requirements?
- Is there a set of requirements agreed to?
- What should you measure?
- What are the steps required to take the input to the output?
- What keeps you from doing the right thing right the first time?
- How can you improve?
- When can it be improved?
- Who can improve it?
- Who owns the process?

As the process is analyzed, the organization starts to understand the horizontal organization within the vertical organization. As ownership for a process or sub-process is assigned, managers realize that organizational survival is accomplished by focusing on the horizontal interaction to benefit the whole.

The benefit will not come immediately. It may take years. However, some immediate results will be apparent within the vertical reporting system. Individual functions will start to understand that it is to their benefit to focus on the entire organization's success and not only on the individual process they own.

A process focus will lead to the following benefits:

- Views work of department as process
- Establishes ownership
- Establishes customer requirements
- Establishes supplier requirements
- Forces agreed-upon set of requirements
- Eliminates non-value-add activities
- Reduces cost of quality
- Uses structured approach for quality improvement
- Improves communication

## Views work of department as process

It is no longer acceptable to reward and recognize managers on the performance of their individual departments. We must add the criteria of performance across the organization on a horizontal basis. Executives and managers must start to understand how each individual department ties together to benefit the entire organization. This is becoming more critical as organizations use matrix type organizational structures.

# Establish ownership

Ownership must be established within our complex organizations. It is no longer acceptable to have organizations functioning without clearly defined ownership for the critical process areas that will determine the survival of the organization.

# Establish customer requirements

Since quality is conformance to customers' requirements, we have to establish what our customer requirements are within the organization. No longer is it acceptable for a function to produce an output and provide it to an organizational customer without determining the requirements of that customer.

# Establish supplier requirements

Individual functions are customers of their supplier. You must meet with the key owner of the input side of the process to determine and communicate your requirements.

# Forces agreed-upon set of requirements

We have built individual kingdoms within organizations. This has led to sub-optimization by departments or individual functions. Instead, we must force the owners of individual functions to sit down with their suppliers and customers and agree on the requirements. This is the first step in eliminating the communications barriers that have been created in organizations over time.

# Eliminates non-value-add activities

Over the years we have built into the processes that we manage many redundant and non-value-add steps. By eliminating non-value-add activity, we directly affect effectiveness and efficiency. Each and every time a non-value-add step is eliminated, we realize productivity the right way.

# Reduces cost of quality

The defect removal cycle will eliminate the cause, not just the symptom. By eliminating the cause, we focus on prevention and reduce failure cost. The main focus is the elimination of defects within, not having to correct them once they are in the output. It is a practical approach to prevention.

# Uses structured approach for quality improvement

Improving quality in white collar environments is not a poster or slogan program with a start and an end. It is a systematic approach to eliminating waste. It requires the use of tools like process analysis and works extremely well in scientific and professional organizations.

# Improves communication

We know there is a direct correlation between good communication and employee morale. As managers and employees work together to increase the effectiveness and efficiency of a process, there is a positive effect on morale. As individual functions start to communicate and focus on their requirements, overall organizational morale increases.

A similar approach to process analysis is currently being used by the U.S. Department of Defense. The Navy has published reference materials on process analysis and value engineering. The fact that an organization as complex as the Defense Department uses a form of process analysis supports the power of this technique in large, complex organizations. However, the technique will also work in state or local government and in educational or medical organizations.

One of the hidden powers of a process focus is that we turn the entire organization in one strategic direction. The power behind this approach is an understanding and an organizational focus on how to achieve excellence with scientific methodology.

One of the major keys to organizational excellence is having all employees understand how the organization will start and continue the journey toward excellence. Constant improvement in an organizational process is one of the techniques that will keep the journey on target.

Process analysis is a methodology that will enable any white collar organization not only to measure quality but also to look at future requirements with a realization of adaptability. The journey to management excellence in white collar environments must be approached both strategically and intellectually. A process focus will allow both to happen, since it provides a methodology for looking within extremely complex organizations and systematically identifies the action required to achieve excellence.

# CHAPTER 5

# QUALITY TEAMS

In my first book, *Quality Circles: Proceed with Caution* (ASQC Quality Press, 1988), I addressed the issue of an alternative to quality circles in white collar environments. I have always been a teacher and practitioner of participative management. However, I strongly feel that it must be tailored to fit the current organizational culture.

Quality teams are in effect the evolution of an effective participative management strategy within the current organization. They should be viewed as a natural outcome of an organization that has effectively practiced participative management.

Teams are a structured approach for looking within the organization to determine the most knowledgeable individuals of how the process works. We constantly move managers from function to function, and many are owners of a sub-process that they have never actually worked in.

This produces a manager responsible for a sub-process without having the in-depth knowledge of the steps required to take the input to the output. However, within their reach of responsibility are individual employees who fully understand the steps required and the ways to eliminate redundant steps and defects.

We must initially select the right employees and, with education, tap this hidden resource. This would have a major impact on helping create a motivational environment to utilize the most important asset in white collar environments: people.

# The management climate

The first step is to determine if the organization is ready for quality teams. This would include a determination of the current participative management climate (see Fig. 5.1).

The participative management chart in Figure 5.1 indicates a left-to-right flow of the six boxes. The key is that the organization must have established an environment for participative management prior to the implementation of teams.

If the management philosophy has been one of delegating and allowing people to be involved in decisions that affect them at work, then we have the start of a participative management environment. A subset of delegation would also be suggestion systems. The next step would have been effective group meetings in which employees shared ideas and concerns. Next would be a task force of some kind and the beginning of a formal structure working as a group on an organizational problem. The mission of a task force is to recommend a solution to management; after that, the task force should dissolve.

The right side of the chart shows the future of participative management and the requirements of a TQM focus.

Following are various types of quality teams.

## Quality improvement team

This group of employees meets on a regular basis in a structured environment to identify a process or project that does not conform to requirements. It is used when you are trying to define the problem.

## Process improvement team

This group of employees meets on a regular basis in a structured environment to identify the current tasks needed to achieve an output. These are employees with the working knowledge of a process who analyze the process, identify defects, and eliminate steps to make the process more effective and efficient. The analysis includes identifying ownership both inside and outside the process; measurements; defects; and requirements for the input and output.

## Project improvement team

This group of employees meets on a regular basis in a structured environment

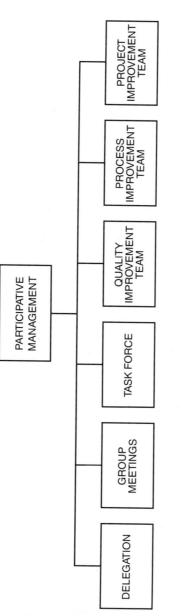

**Figure 5.1: Participative management structure**

to focus on a specific project. This includes the elimination of defects in a process. This could be a spinoff of the process improvement team.

If the current organizational culture is one of preaching participative management while practicing something entirely different, teams will not work.

Team deterioration can also be attributed to:

- Area of focus
- Structure
- Lack of success
- Training/communications
- Unrealistic expectations
- Not understanding the entire process
- Problems within groups
- Decrease in management support
- Lack of recognition

## Area of focus

The quality teams are not focusing on important issues which affect the business. In so doing, the group is not able to attract management interest, and therefore gets neither sufficient support nor recognition.

## Structure

The team is not structured well, and neither responsibility nor ownership has been assigned.

## Lack of success

No plans were in place to ensure success. The quality teams' activities are looked upon as programs with a start and an end, rather than as continuous quality improvement.

## Training/communication

Inadequate training was provided. The training should include group dynamics and logical problem-solving techniques. It should also include complete communication on how teams are structured and what their mission is.

## Unrealistic expectations

Unattainable targets were set for the members. You do not try to fix the organization's problems all at once. Management may have unrealistic expectations that teams will fix the entire organization, rather than understanding that they are only one tool in an organization's journey to management excellence.

## Not understanding the entire process

Members have not been instructed in basic process analysis and do not understand the importance of effectiveness prior to efficiency.

## Problems within groups

Members are not informed on how well they can contribute toward the team's efforts. They look upon the team as an additional workload, which makes them feel less enthusiastic. Leaders or managers have not selected the right members for the team. Individuals who are dissatisfied with their responsibilities, their manager, or the company may use the meeting as a forum for complaints.

## Decrease in management support

Managers do not understand that this is a journey, not a destination. They become focused on a quick fix rather than on constant quality improvement.

## Lack of recognition

Behavior that gets rewarded gets repeated. If quality team members are not recognized for their efforts and contributions, they can easily fail. The key is to create a motivational environment that supports this subset of participative management.

Quality teams are structured specifically for white collar environments and accept ownership for the solution. They understand the importance of working on key issues within the organization, not on nuisances.

The team structures would be as follows:

- Select volunteers
- Training
- Task focus
- Focus on "group think" prevention
- 1½ hour duration once a week
- Start on time, end on time
- Take minutes
- Publicize minutes and team efforts
- Communicate and recognize success

Teams are also a method of creating an environment that can lead to innovation and creativity. If techniques teach logical problem solving, we are focusing on using the complete mental ability of employees, not just a small piece.

We must develop a logical sequence of problem solving that can be transferred to the daily work environment and not just used in the team sessions. By using a logical problem solving technique, we get the hidden benefit of teams, which is employee and management development.

This hidden benefit can produce results within an organization that will contribute to organizational excellence. An organization that creates an environment that develops employees and managers will benefit on a long-term basis, since quality happens through people in white collar environments.

One approach to team problem solving is as follows:

1. Analyze the process.
2. Brainstorm three key areas (People/Materials/Procedures).
3. Use the 80/20 rule.
4. Analyze the problem which has been selected.
5. Decide what facts are needed to solve the problem.
6. Gather data about the problem.
7. Interpret the data that has been collected.
8. Devise a solution to the problem based on the facts.
9. Prepare and present the solution.
10. Implement the solution.
11. Monitor and document results.

Another team or individual technique that can contribute to creating an organizational environment for employee and management development is the five-stage problem solving process.

# The five-stage PSP

The five-stage problem solving process (PSP) is a well-thought-out technique. It provides a structured approach for working on a problem from the stage where a symptom is observed through the stage where a solution is identified and implemented. Improvement is realized and appropriately integrated into the system as part of the continuous improvement effort that is badly needed in white collar environments.

Problems that we encounter in the day-to-day operation of an organization may surface from various activities, such as: when teams are formed during process analysis, during routine business transactions, routine customer surveys, and management reports; and in critical business situations where management attention is called for.

Such problems can be resolved in many ways (see Fig. 5.2), either through management intervention, individual action, or collective actions by a team of people with expertise and skills in that area. In any of these approaches, the use of a similarly structured approach will increase the rate of success in problem resolution and attainment of improvement desired. The results are an improvement in the area of ownership for one's output, giving more value with the same input value leading to customer loyalty, better organizational reputation and effectiveness, efficiency, and adaptability.

| Problem Sources | Five-Stage Process | Quality Improvement |
|---|---|---|
| Management/Department Planning Sessions Quality Teams | Identify/Define | Superior Ownership <br> • Less Rework <br> • Fewer Errors |
| Process Analysis | Analyze Cause | Higher Customer Loyalty: a better job of exceeding customer expectations |
| Day-To-Day Activities <br> • Performance report <br> • Surveys <br> • Customer inputs | Set Targets | Improved: <br> • Effectiveness <br> • Efficiency <br> • Adaptability |
| Urgent Management Request | Solve/Implement | |
| | Measure/Track/ Control | |

**Figure 5.2   An overview of the five-stage PSP**

Figure 5.3 shows an overall view of the five-stage PSP. Each of the five stages is designed to produce answers to the questions shown. Answering such questions carefully at each stage will result in an effective and efficient process. It will often be necessary to backtrack and rework at a previous stage, but this can be minimized by reviewing some key suggestions.

The common causes of ineffective problem solving are as follows:

- People jumped to solutions before the problem was really defined; they worked on the symptom that they saw and felt.
- People made assumptions about certain conditions and the causes without checking the validity of such assumptions and the possible correlation with the symptom observed.
- People failed to identify a measurement plan with data obtainable to indicate if the action is effective otherwise.
- People don't have the perseverance to track and observe the changes.

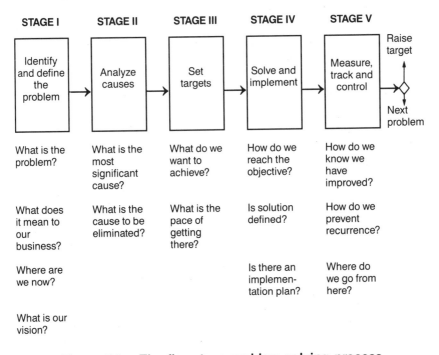

**Figure 5.3:    The five-stage problem-solving process**

Adhering to the principles of the PSP will minimize the occurrence of those deficiencies. It is particularly important to spend sufficient time in stages I and II to establish a sound footing for the solutions and implementation that follow. Experience indicates these two stages take the most time and effort.

People tend to give up trying at these early stages, for their efforts are not realized and easily seen by management. Because things are moving so quickly, the focus may be changed and the emphasis is not sustained to see through these two early stages. Stages I and II can take up more than half the total PSP time, because it is here that a thorough analysis of current conditions takes place. This is also the time when data must be collected and analyzed to support or refute the assumptions people made in the process of solving the problem.

Stage III is a critical point in the process. It is here that quantitative targets are set that will measure the success of the solutions and implementation plans defined in stage IV. Finally, stage V is where the actual execution, measurement, and tracking take place, along with the final evaluation and decision-making.

This approach of problem solving for the nonmanufacturing environment employs a series of expansion and contraction techniques at stages I, II, and IV. The expansion part of the corresponding stage is the infusion of many ideas from many sources or people in the team who have different perspectives on the problem.

Repeated environments and exercises reveal that no single one of us is as smart as all of us. This opening-up process allows the consideration of divergent points of view from members of a team. The contraction part of the corresponding stage is where use of certain selection processes enables the list of ideas to be narrowed down to a single issue so that effort can be devoted to it.

In general, the expansion part uses the creative thinking process that leads to a list of possible ideas. Brainstorming is one of the most practical methods to apply. Data analysis, with the use of techniques such as tally sheets, scattered diagrams, statistics, and to a large extent business judgment, is to be adopted in the contraction phase. This series of expansions and contractions occurs repetitively along the five-stage problem solving process.

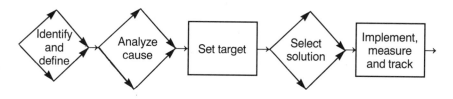

**Figure 5.4: Idea generation and selection**

This technique encourages development of innovation. The innovative solution is the answer to the problems we face each day in running a business or using limited organizational resources. All conventional approaches, if available, have been dreamed of and tested long ago. Such innovation provides enough structure to avoid confusion, yet offers enough freedom to allow for spontaneity. Figure 5.4 shows how the input and output of stages III and V relate to the expansion-contraction concept just described.

In white collar environments, we must use educational techniques and provide knowledge that will contribute to a motivational environment to produce organizational excellence.

Quality teams provided with effective problem solving techniques can play a major role in future organizational survival.

Our knowledge of how the human brain functions is limited. However, we do know that we can develop the brain by teaching techniques that facilitate whole-brain thinking. We also know that we solve problems by a process of divergent and convergent thinking. We go away from the problem, gather additional information, then diverge back for the solution.

If we are looking for creativity and innovation, the place to find it is within the organization, not outside.

We must instruct employees in techniques such as the five-stage PSP and brainstorming. This will result in a change of behavior and create an environment so that people within organizations can become creative and innovative.

Teams are a subset of a systematic, strategic process to excellence. They support and play a major role in an organization's journey to excellence. However, if they are not considered in a strategic manner, they can cause more harm than good.

The decision to use teams must be both an operational and a strategic decision.

They are not an approach to be tried merely because other organizations are using them effectively. Teams must be looked upon as part of a whole; the whole is the entire strategic process to excellence.

Teams can help or hurt an organization's journey toward excellence. It all depends on how management decides to implement them.

# CHAPTER 6

# TAKING OWNERSHIP FOR TOTAL QUALITY MANAGEMENT

Taking ownership for TQM is a decision made in the management pyramid. It starts at the executive level and flows down the entire organization. It is a strategic, not an operational decision. It is a decision that says we will take ownership for TQM and will drive it within the organization. It is a decision that says we will walk our talk, we will practice what we preach. This is not a program with a start and an end. It is a total organizational commitment to excellence to be followed by all.

What we are really focusing on is an evolution of all the good things that have worked in management, packaged under a total organizational commitment. It is a systematic, strategic approach to organizational excellence using a practical management technique. It is the practical application of quality deployment in white collar quality environments.

The starting point is for management to ask some key questions:

- Are you willing to change your organization?
- Will you create the environment for change?
- Will you train others and commit resources for that purpose?

- Will you demonstrate commitment by your action?
- Will you positively reinforce progress?

The questions are not easy to answer, since they require more than a decision that is delegated down the organization. What these questions require is a management commitment to change the way we manage. This is probably one of the most difficult decisions an organization will have to make.

Complacency is death, whether it be at an individual management level or an organizational level. Complacency comes when we sit back and say, "We are doing great." Instead, we require constant quality improvement.

The first step is a process focus which looks at TQM as a process in itself (see Fig. 6.1).

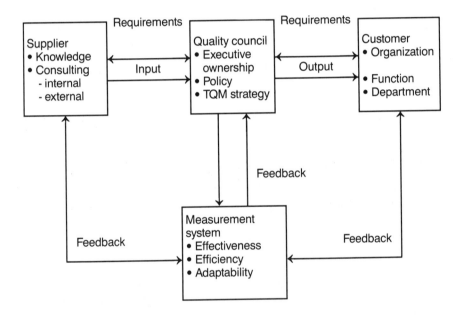

**Figure 6.1:   The TQM Process**

An executive quality council must be formed to develop a vision and strategy for the organization. The vision must be articulated to the entire organization and should be tailored to the current organizational culture. Such programs have a variety of names in various organizations and cultures:

Excellence—IBM
Managing Total Quality (MTQ)—3M
Total Quality Control—Hewlett-Packard
Q+—ARMCO
Quality Improvement Program—FP&L
EQIP—Ethyl Corporation

Leadership Through Quality — Xerox
Quality Process — First National Bank of Chicago
Total Quality Management System — Corning
Quality First — Ford
TQC and CWQC — Japan

The important factor is not what you call the program but what you do with it. It cannot become a management fad tied to a particular government administration or CEO. It is a commitment by the management team to constant organizational quality improvement.

It is a commitment supported by a management checklist:

- I discuss quality in my daily conversations.
- I insert quality messages in my presentation.
- I require quality as part of performance appraisals and reviews.
- I review quality in various aspects of my job.
- I commit resources to promote quality in my organization.

A manager's quality commitment checklist answers the question: Are you practicing what you preach? It is more than using quality terms; it is incorporating them into action that will take the organization on its journey to management excellence.

A TQM strategy must be developed for each individual organization and culture. There is no one laundry list that will apply to all organizations. However, Figure 6.2 shows a road map that we developed for the Federal Quality Institute full-day course. This chart and the following charts are given to senior executive service employees of the federal government who attend the TQM course.

The journey follows these steps:

**Step 1: Your present management and measurement system.**
- Analyze your present measurement system
- Customer-driven
- Supplier-driven

**Step 2: Assess your unique operation or organization.**
- Current structure
- Organizational culture
- Quality culture

**Step 3: Executive commitment to TQM.**
- Ownership

**Step 4: Create vision and philosophy.**
- Strategic
- Innovative

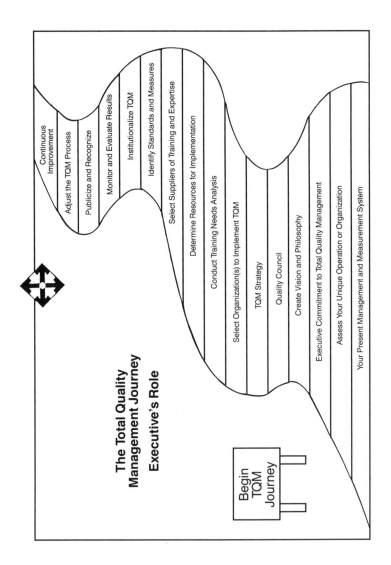

**The Total Quality
Management Journey**

**Executive's Role**

Continuous Improvement

Adjust the TQM Process

Publicize and Recognize

Monitor and Evaluate Results

Institutionalize TQM

Identify Standards and Measures

Select Suppliers of Training and Expertise

Determine Resources for Implementation

Conduct Training Needs Analysis

Select Organization(s) to Implement TQM

TQM Strategy

Quality Council

Create Vision and Philosophy

Executive Commitment to Total Quality Management

Assess Your Unique Operation or Organization

Your Present Management and Measurement System

Begin TQM Journey

**Figure 6.2   The roadmap to excellence**

### Step 5: Quality council.
- Set quality goals, statement of commitment, objectives, and measurement for success
- Select key executive level process ownership

### Step 6: TQM strategy.
- Systematic strategic process for excellence
- Quality deployment

### Step 7: Select organization(s) to implement TQM.
- Current organization's performance
- Key process for organizational survival

### Step 8: Conduct training needs analysis.
- Attitude behavior required
- Skills required

### Step 9: Determine resources for implementation.
- Internal resources
- External resources

### Step 10: Select suppliers of training and expertise.
- Organizations that fit your unique culture
- Proven experience in your unique environment

### Step 11: Identify standards and measures.
- Constant quality improvement
- Process-driven
- Effectiveness
- Efficiency
- Adaptability

### Step 12: Institutionalize TQM.
- Driven by organization, not an individual
- Becomes the culture
- Business as usual

### Step 13: Monitor and evaluate results.
- Feedback system
- Communications

### Step 14: Publicize and recognize.
- Constant recognition of the journey
- Reinforce behavior

### Step 15: Adjust the TQM process.
- Fine-tune.
- Refine as required

### Step 16: Continuous improvement.
- It never ends

TQM requires a strategy that will vary by organization. There is no one answer or approach to management excellence. My experience has led me to conclude that a quality focus must be tailored to each individual organization. One organization will tell me that it is following one specific quality expert's recommendation while another takes an entirely different approach.

I have concluded that what is required is to choose and pick from all the experts to determine what will work in specific organizations. When we look at the recommendations of some of the world leaders in quality (W. Edwards Deming, Joseph Juran, Philip Crosby, and Armand Feigenbaum), we see some agreement on these points:

1. Producing a quality product or service costs less because there is less waste.
2. Preventing quality problems is better than detecting and correcting them.
3. Statistical data should be used to measure quality.
4. Managers need to take a leadership role in improving quality.
5. Managers and employees need training in quality improvement.
6. Companies need to develop a quality management system.

The organization that starts on this journey must realize that it requires a management system in place to achieve management excellence. All the training in the world will not make it happen if there is no management system in place to manage it.

A management system includes the assignment of the role managers will play in this journey (see Fig. 6.3). As a manager, you should:

- Seek advice from individuals (internal or external to your organization) who are knowledgeable in TQM.
- Educate your immediate managers in TQM.
- Develop an organizational quality improvement plan.
- Orient managers to TQM.
- Orient employees to TQM.
- Select a work process for improvement.
- Identify the customers' and suppliers' requirements for that work process.
- Set a method for selecting quality improvement teams.
- Form quality improvement teams.
- Train teams.
- Monitor and measure team progress.
- Publicize and reward results.
- Continue to improve work process.
- Start over again with a new process for improvement.

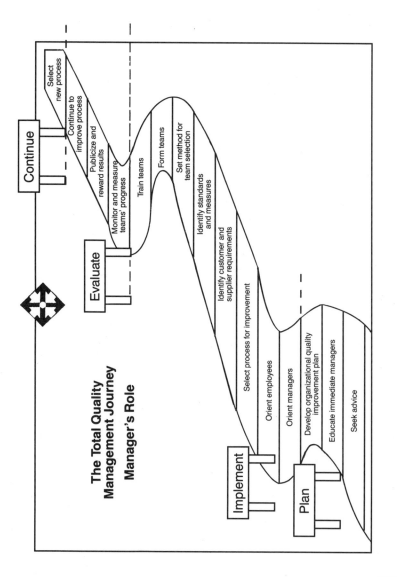

**Figure 6.3: Educational strategy**

This logical sequence of events is tailored to each individual function and is directed to constant quality improvement.

The ownership for TQM comes in management making a total commitment to excellence. It is accepting ownership that nothing will happen within the organization until management decides to make it happen.

Organizations that survive in a limited-resources environment are organizations that have placed quality as a priority and have it as a survival strategy. As part of this survival strategy, they fully understand the importance of providing the right knowledge to all employees. They fully understand that knowledge is power and must be approached in a strategic manner under the management system.

Before any knowledge in quality is given to any employee in an organization, the organization needs analysis must be conducted. The needs analysis can be accomplished in a number of ways:

- Individual interviews
- Group interviews
- Questionnaires and surveys

Once the needs analysis is conducted, an educational strategy can be developed that communicates the role of each level of the organization and ownership (see Fig. 6.4).

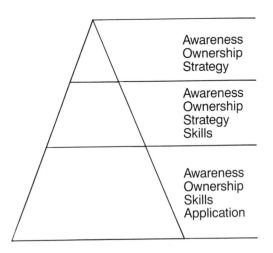

Awareness/Ownership/Skills/Application

**Figure 6.4:  Educational strategy**

# Strategy at each level

At the top of the pyramid we are dealing with the smallest percentage of the entire organizational structure—less than one percent. However, it is at this level that the journey starts. This is the level that must start the vision and the systematic, strategic process for organizational excellence.

The educational knowledge that should be provided to this level is no more than a day in quality awareness. It should be knowledge structured specifically for executive levels with their direct reporting teams. At this level the most effective approach is to educate executives in family groups of their organization.

Training in family groups should provide the environment and opportunity to define how this approach will fit their unique culture and organization. It will also start the executive team in the direction of developing its unique implementation strategy. The focus of the knowledge should be on giving them a clear understanding that they must take personal ownership for the strategic approach to excellence.

The middle level of management should receive a form of awareness training in combination with some skills training. This is the type of training that will allow them to support the systematic, strategic process for excellence that was developed at the executive level. It will also clearly define their roles in the implementation of excellence deployment.

At this level, the knowledge must be packaged to hook them. It must clearly show why they should support this approach and not another management technique. They must be given the knowledge that communicates the level of top commitment and the fact that this will become an organizational strategy. If possible, middle managers should also be trained in family groups and given some type of exercise that will assist them with the implementation of an excellence strategy.

We now come to the base of the pyramid, the first-line managers and the employees who report to them. At the first-line manager level, knowledge should focus on skills and practical application. Managers should be instructed in the specific management skills they will need to implement the strategy. However, the skills they are provided with should also focus on management techniques for excellence.

At the base, we reach the largest population of the organization, and it is at this level that we come to the moment of truth. This level will deal directly with the organization's customers, and it is at this level that the entire pyramid must focus to achieve the buy-in.

It is at this level that the greatest investment in knowledge will be required. The organization must clearly define what skills currently exist and what skills will be required.

Awareness training at this level can be conducted in large groups of employees. The awareness training should not only communicate the basics of quality but should also demonstrate management's commitment to excellence.

Once awareness knowledge has been given, we can conduct skills and applications training. If possible, this training should be conducted in family groups with the first-line manager. The objective of this approach is to determine how employees will use the newly-acquired skills within their immediate manager's function.

# Concept of ownership

One main theme that will be given in this educational strategy is the concept of ownership. It will be repeated over and over again and directly tied in to the systematic, strategic process for excellence. It is an organizational strategic approach to knowledge. The objective is to have the entire organization heading in the same direction on a journey toward excellence.

The focus must be on quality, which is the practical manifestation of excellence, and there is no alternative for organizational survival. At the worker level, we need to develop the type of ownership that produces the old craftsman mentality in the work output. This attitude and behavior can be transferred to white collar environments if management will only take ownership for management excellence with a focus on quality improvement.

The major lesson I have learned in the field of white collar quality, which applies worldwide in all cultures in both public and private sectors, is that employees will take ownership if management takes the lead in action and not just words. The issue of managers not taking the lead confuses me, since that is their role and that is what they are paid to do.

# People managers successful

It appears that the most successful managers in white collar quality turn out to be managers who have strong human resource skills. People managers not only quickly understand the power behind a quality focus but also understand that it happens through the people in the organization and that it starts with management. They understand that it cannot be delegated and must come directly from them with their behavior.

People managers understand that a majority of the work force want to identify with a quality organization and a quality work output. They also understand that this is not a typical program with a specific stop time. A program communicates a period of time; a management excellence focus means constant, never-ending quality improvement.

We are facing extremely difficult times in both public- and private-sector nonmanufacturing environments. It will require that the people managers take ownership for quality in their own organizations and drive it with a number one priority. They then become missionaries of the quality message within the major organization and convince other managers by their excellent achievements that there is no alternative. The message starts to spread within the organization as other managers realize that this is not another management fad but a natural evolution of the historical proven techniques of management. This evolution had to come, and it is here now. The organizations, both public and private, that do not focus on a strategic methodology to achieve excellence will not survive.

# CHAPTER 7

# THE ISSUE AND SOLUTION

The issue that both private and public organizations are facing today is one of focus. Due to our educational experiences, we have had a major focus on the productivity side of the formula for human potential, not on the waste side. Productivity is only a measurement, not reality. We must refocus our efforts in the area of waste.

Over the years during presentations to various public and private audiences, I have used the following formula:

---

**Human Potential = Productivity + Waste**

---

# Using the human resource

Assuming that human potential is 100 percent, I ask various groups of managers and executives: what is the current overall average utilization of the human potential within your organization? The response I get is that it is anywhere from 50 percent to 65 percent. To look at it from the formula standpoint, it would become:

## Effective Utilization
## of Human Potential = Productivity − Waste

I then ask them what percentage of their organizational expense they spend in the area of human resources. Again, their response is that anywhere from 50 percent to 65 percent of total organizational expense is spent on human resources.

Here is the issue. The most expensive resource of the organization is only being utilized at 50 percent to 65 percent of its potential.

Another way to look at it is that we are 100 percent efficient/productive doing rework. The next logical question is, who is responsible for this? The answer is complete silence.

Management has focused its attention mainly on productivity, not on waste. In addition, management must accept ownership for the current unacceptable utilization of the human resource in our organizations.

When managers start to realize they are responsible for waste in organizations, we can begin the journey toward management excellence.

We have built extremely complex organizations with all types of support and measurement systems to focus on an output called productivity. We constantly measure the output year after year and make all types of organizational comparisons. We make the incorrect assumption that if productivity increases by a predetermined percentage, we are in great shape. We have not focused on the process that takes us to this measurement of productivity. When we step back and start to examine the process, not the outcome, we realize the waste component is preventing us from achieving a higher or incremental improvement in the utilization of the human resource.

Our focus should be on eliminating waste within the organization while maintaining some reasonable measures of productivity. I am not advocating a discontinuance of organizational productivity measurements. What I am advocating is a refocus on waste.

We can no longer manage public and private sector organizations with expense items that can represent up to 50 percent of gross expense, with the organizations performing at 60 percent of potential. If we continue with this performance while only focusing on absolute productivity then the organization must fail—and it should. Management must take the responsibility for its failure.

I have seen organization after organization celebrate an achievement in the area of a productivity measurement. Many management reward and recognition systems are tied to achieving an increase in a productivity measurement. This celebration is going on while the organization is utilizing its most important and costly resource at approximately 60 percent of its potential.

It appears that Western managers are trained and educated to focus on the productivity result while the organization is experiencing serious waste within the process. The waste is not a result of the lack of concern on the part of management; it is due to a lack of focus.

# Refocus on waste

TQM allows us to refocus management's attention on the waste side of the formula. It is nothing more than a strategic and operational approach to eliminating waste within the organization.

The journey toward a solution starts and ends with education. Providing knowledge to managers and executives creates an environment in which they can start the journey toward management excellence.

One example of a large organization's commitment to providing this knowledge is the federal government. In 1988, the federal government created the Federal Quality Institute. Its mission is to provide quality awareness training courses to federal government management teams. The one-day course provides executives and managers with the information they need to decide whether to begin the TQM journey. The basic agenda of the one-day course is:

- Introduction
- Historical perspective
- Total quality management
- Overview of quality
- Teams
- Team practical assignment
- Successful examples in the government
- Taking ownership for quality

# Introduction

The class size is usually limited to 30 participants in a family group from a specific agency or executive department. Its seating arrangement is set in a U shape to facilitate discussion and participation. The instructors are members of the senior executive service who are on a one-year rotational assignment at the Federal Quality Institute. They have been placed on loan by a specific executive department or agency and will return to that executive department or agency and become the focal person for knowledge on TQM. The objective of the course is to provide senior executives with an understanding of how TQM can be employed to accomplish their quality and productivity improvement objectives.

# Historical perspective

This section reviews the history of past presidential administrations' efforts to increase quality and productivity in the federal government. Reference is also made to the various executive orders from the president and directives from the executive office on quality and productivity.

# Total quality management

In this segment, the following principles are introduced:

- Meeting customer requirements
- Making continuous improvement
- Giving everyone responsibility for quality
- Using a strategic process

# Overview of quality

This segment provides a complete overview of the concepts of quality, including the following definition: quality is a product or service that meets customer requirements and is fit for use. A total quality model for meeting customer requirements is introduced:

- A focus on the customer
  —Quality
  —Customer/supplier relationships
- Effective and renewed communications
  —Purpose
  —Elements
- Reliance on standards and measures
  —Roles
  —Pitfalls

A complete section is also dedicated to making continuous improvement, and there is an introduction to using a process focus. The cost of quality is also introduced, along with various problem-solving techniques.

# Teams

In this section, the executive's role in taking ownership is introduced, in addition to organizational and quality cultures. Teams are introduced as a recommendation to effectively implement the future of participative management.

# Team practical assignment

Here is a value-add hands-on section in which participants apply some of the knowledge they have learned with practice and feedback.

**Knowledge + Practice + Feedback = Success**

They are divided into teams of five to six members and asked to work on the implementing TQM workshop. They must identify the driving and restraining forces to implementing TQM in their organization and decide what steps they can take back to their organizations to implement TQM. They use such techniques as brainstorming, nominal group technique, and force field analysis. Each team appoints a spokesperson who presents the team's findings and recommendations to the entire class. The presentation charts are collected and typed, then given to the executive head of the organization.

# Successful examples in the government

There have been numerous success stories on this approach within the federal government. This information is shared, and a central resource center for additional information and knowledge on quality and productivity is made available.

# Taking ownership for quality

The last section of the course focuses on taking executive ownership for TQM. It communicates the importance of executive action rather than words. It clearly defines, with supporting charts, how to develop a systematic, strategic process for excellence.

The Federal Quality Institute executive TQM course is a practical approach to the journey toward excellence. It provides participants with real-world experience in both the public and private sectors. The fact that the instructors are peers of the participants, not academic lecturers with no practical experience, adds to the credibility of the knowledge provided. One of the hidden benefits of this approach is that the federal government has realized that is has the dedicated, knowledgeable individuals within its own culture to solve its own problems. The fact that senior executive services members are the instructors is a compliment to the federal government.

# Solving from within

Here is a perfect example of how organizations must solve their own problems from within. They require some outside knowledge and assistance to get the journey started. However, once the journey is started, they must take ownership for it. Another benefit of the federal government's effort to providing strategic knowledge for excellence is that it builds networks within the government. Such networks help to reinforce individual change agents within the various organizations. They start to share knowledge and experience, and they help each other implement excellence.

This effort by the federal government is the beginning of the solution to the issue. It is my opinion that this effort will spread to state and local governments as organizations realize that absolute productivity is not the answer when tackled with limited resources.

Here we have a major effort underway within the federal government that was initiated by the fact that a productivity focus is not the solution. Waste elimination must become the focus in all organizations.

When we look within the organizations we manage, it is easy to see the productivity trap. In many organizations it has almost become a numbers game: give members of higher management the numbers that they are looking for, and the pressure will be off. However, as we play the numbers game, organizational performance can be headed for a serious fall.

A majority of managers are dedicated, hard-working individuals. They are searching for a methodology that will allow them to balance effectiveness and efficiency. Managers have been exposed to a never-ending list of approaches and techniques to accomplish their tasks. It is no wonder they seem skeptical when another approach is recommended. However, a TQM approach allows them to take the best of various techniques that have worked and produce an overall strategy. Such a management strategy will increase the effective utilization of human resources on an incremental basis over time. It provides techniques to revisit the way organizations function and to use scientific approaches to eliminate defects within the organization.

A structured approach to excellence allows an organization to start on a journey that can only result in benefits to all employees. As this environment starts to change, the organization changes. It is the type of change that is not forced upon the organization by external forces but comes from within. This change occurs because the organization is able to anticipate what is required in a proactive mode, not remain in a reactive mode.

Organizational survival starts with the understanding that reacting to environments is no longer acceptable. Organizations must become proactive, and that can only happen if the organization has a strategy to produce an organizational culture that is proactive. Our organizational focus must change, since the world is changing around us. We have devoted a great deal of effort and time to changing our manufacturing environments while overlooking the fact that the future is also in the hands of our white collar environments.

Managers agree that we must increase the utilization of our white collar population. The only disagreement seems to be in the name selected for this strategic approach. The solution is not in what you call it; the solution is in what you do with it.

Excellence is a moving target, and organizations that hit the target have done so by a strategic process. Such a process clearly defines and communicates to all employees the methodology that will be used to achieve excellence.

A strategic process communicates the mission, goals, and objectives, and the methodologies to achieve them. It is a scientific approach to managing the organization, with a built-in constant incremental improvement strategy. The improvement is in each individual process as it is managed toward its result. However, the main management focus is on the process with its journey, not on the specific results of the process.

Since we live in a society that is extremely results-oriented, it will not be easy to refocus our attention. It will require a reeducation process of all levels of management to establish a systematic, strategic process to achieve excellence.

A systematic, strategic process for organizational excellence must be developed at the top of the pyramid at the executive level. It must then be communicated down the pyramid to all levels of management and eventually to all employees.

The issue is our current organizational focus on results and measurements. The solution is to focus on the journey and constant incremental improvement while keeping an eye on the results.

**BIBLIOGRAPHY**

Albrecht, Karl, and Ron Zemke. *Service America! Doing Business in the New Economy.* Homewood, Ill.: Dow Jones-Irwin, 1985.

ASQC Quality Costs Committee. *Principles of Quality Costs.* John T. Hagan, ed. Milwaukee: ASQC Quality Press, 1986.

Barry, Thomas J. *Quality Circles: Proceed with Caution.* Milwaukee: ASQC Quality Press, 1988.

Bellman, Geoffrey M. *The Quest for Staff Leadership.* Glenview, Ill.: Scott Foresman & Co., 1985.

Block, Peter. *Flawless Consulting.* San Diego: University Association, 1981.

Bradford, Cohen. *Managing for Excellence.* New York: John Wiley & Sons, 1984.

Brassard, Michael, ed. *The Memory Jogger.* Lawrence, Mass.: GOAL (Growth Opportunity Alliance of Greater Lawrence), 1985.

Burr, Irving W. *Elementary Statistical Quality Control.* New York: Marcel Dekker, Inc., 1979.

Clark, Kim B., Robert H. Hayes, and Christopher Lorenz. *The Uneasy Alliance: Managing the Productivity-Technology Dilemma.* Boston: Harvard Business School Press, 1985.

Cochran, William G. *Sampling Techniques.* 3d ed. New York: John Wiley & Sons, 1977.

Crosby, Philip B. *Quality Is Free: The Art of Making Quality Certain.* New York: New American Library, 1979.

_____. *Quality Without Tears: The Art of Hassle-Free Management.* New York: New American Library, 1984.

_____. *Running Things: The Art of Making Things Happen.* New York: New American Library, 1986.

Deming, W. Edwards. *Out of the Crisis.* Cambridge, Mass.: MIT Center for Advanced Engineering Study, 1986.

_____. *Quality, Productivity and Competitive Position.* Cambridge, Mass.: MIT Center for Advanced Engineering Study, 1982.

Drucker, Peter F. *The Frontiers of Management.* New York: New American Library, 1986.

Federal Quality Institute. *Senior Executive Service Total Quality Management Course.* Office of Personnel Management, Washington, D.C., 1988.

Feigenbaum, Armand V. *Total Quality Control.* 3d ed. New York: McGraw-Hill Book Co., 1983.

Ford, Henry. *Today and Tomorrow.* Garden City, NY: Doubleday, Page & Co., 1926.

FPL QualTech. *FPL Quality Improvement Program: Guidebook and Roadmap.* Florida Power and Light, 1984.

Fukuda, Ryuji. *Managerial Engineering.* Cambridge, Mass.: Productivity Press, 1984.

Garfield, Charles A. *Peak Performance: The New Heroes of American Business.* New York: William Morrow, 1986.

Gitlow, Howard S., and Shelly J. Gitlow. *The Deming Guide to Quality and Competitive Position.* Englewood Cliffs, NJ: Prentice Hall Inc., 1987.

Gordon, Thomas. *Effective Leader Training E.L.T.* New York: Bantam Books, 1978.

Grayson, C. Jackson, and Carla O'Dell. *American Business—A Two Minute Warning.* New York: McMillan Free Press, 1988.

Guaspari, John. *I Know It When I See It.* New York: American Management Association, 1985.

Harrington, H. James. *Excellence—the IBM Way.* Milwaukee: ASQC Quality Press, 1988.

_____. *The Improvement Process: How America's Leading Companies Improve Quality.* Milwaukee: ASQC Quality Press, 1987.

_____. *Poor-Quality Cost.* Milwaukee: ASQC Quality Press, 1987.

Ishikawa, Kaoru. *Guide to Quality Control.* 2d ed. Tokyo: Asian Productivity Organization, 1985.

_____. *What Is Total Quality Control? The Japanese Way.* Englewood Cliffs, NJ: Prentice Hall, Inc., 1985.

Japan Human Relations Association, ed. *The Idea Book.* Cambridge, Mass.: Productivity Press, 1988.

Johnson, Ross H., and Richard T. Weber. *Buying Quality.* Milwaukee: ASQC Quality Press, 1985.

Juran, Joseph M. *Managerial Breakthrough.* New York: McGraw-Hill Book Co., 1964.

_____. *Quality Control Handbook.* 3d ed. New York: McGraw-Hill Book Co., 1980.

Juran, Joseph M., and Frank M. Gryna. *Quality Planning and Analysis.* 2d ed. New York: McGraw-Hill Book Co., 1980.

Kane, Edward J. "IBM's Quality Focus on the Business Process." *Quality Progress* (April 1986): 26-33.

Kanter, Rosabeth Moss. *Change Masters—Innovation for Productivity in the American Corporation.* New York: Simon & Schuster, 1983.

Karatsu, Hajime. *TQC Wisdom of Japan.* Cambridge, Mass.: Productivity Press, 1988.

Keirsey, David, and Marilyn Bates. *Please Understand Me—Character & Temperament Types.* Delmar, Calif.: Prometheus Nemesis, 1978.

Kilian, Cecilia S. *The World of W. Edwards Deming.* Washington, D.C.: CEEPress Books, 1988.

Kume, Hitoshi. *Statistical Methods for Quality Improvement.* Tokyo: The Association for Overseas Technical Scholarship, 1985.

Latzko, William J. *Quality and Productivity for Bankers and Financial Managers.* Milwaukee: ASQC Quality Press, 1986.

Lawler, Edward E., III. *High Involvement Management.* San Francisco: Jossey Bass, 1986.

Lu, David J. *Inside Corporate Japan—The Art of Fumble-Free Management.* Cambridge, Mass.: Productivity Press, 1987.

Maass, Richard A. *World Class Quality: An Innovative Prescription for Survival.* Milwaukee: ASQC Quality Press, 1988.

McGregor, D.M. *The Human Side of Enterprise.* New York: McGraw-Hill Book Co., 1960.

Mager, Robert F., and Peter Pipe. *Analyzing Performance Problems.* Belmont, Calif.: Fearon Pitman Publishers, 1970.

Mann, Nanavy R. *The Keys of Excellence—The Story of the Deming Philosophy.* Los Angeles: Prestwick Books, 1987.

Meier, Kenneth J., and Jeffrey L. Brundney. *Applied Statistics for Public Administration.* Boston: Duxbury Press, 1981.

Michalak, Donald Fry, and Edwin G. Yager. *Making the Training Process Work.* New York: Harper & Row, 1979.

Myers, Isabel Briggs. *Gifts Differing.* Palo Alto, Calif.: Consulting Psychology Press, 1980.

Pall, Gabriel. *Quality Process Management.* Englewood Cliffs, NJ: Prentice Hall, 1987.

Peters, Thomas J., and Nancy Austin. *A Passion for Excellence: The Leadership Difference.* New York: Random House, 1985.

Peters, Thomas J., and Robert H. Waterman. *In Search of Excellence: Lessons from America's Best-Run Companies.* New York: Harper and Row, 1982.

Peters, Thomas J. *Thriving on Chaos.* New York: Knopf, 1987.

Pinchot, Gifford. *Intrapreneuring.* New York: Harper & Row, 1985.

Prokesch, Steven E. "Bean Meshes Man, Machine." *The New York Times* (December 23, 1985).

Pyzdek, Thomas. *An SPC Primer.* Tucson, Ariz.: Quality America Inc., 1985.

Rosander, A. C. *Applications of Quality Control in the Service Industries.* Milwaukee: ASQC Quality Press, 1985.

Scherkenbach, William. *The Deming Route to Quality and Productivity: Roadmaps and Roadblocks.* Rockville, Md.: Mercury Press, 1986.

Schrock, Edward M, and Henry L. Lefevre. *The Good and the Bad News About Quality.* Milwaukee: ASQC Quality Press, 1988.

Shewhart, Walter A. *Economic Control of Quality of Manufactured Product.* Milwaukee: ASQC Quality Press, 1980.

_____. *Statistical Method from the Viewpoint of Quality Control.* Washington, D.C.: Department of Agriculture, 1939.

Shores, A. Richard. *Survival of the Fittest.* Milwaukee: ASQC Quality Press, 1988.

Skinner, Wickham. "The Productivity Paradox." *Harvard Business Review.* (July/August, 1986): 55-59.

Stockton, John R., and Charles T. Clark. *Introduction to Business and Economic Statistics.* 5d ed. Ohio: South-Western Publishing Co., 1985.

Stratton, A. Donald. *An Approach to Quality Improvement that Works—With an Emphasis on the White-Collar Area.* Milwaukee: ASQC Quality Press, 1988.

Torbeck, Lynn D. "A Bibliography of Quality in the Service Industries." *Quality Progress* (June 1985): 74-83.

Townsend, Patrick L. *Commit to Quality.* New York: John Wiley & Sons, 1986.

Von Oech, Roger. *A Whack on the Side of the Head, A Kick in the Seat of the Pants.* New York: Warner Books, Inc., 1983.

Walton, Mary. *The Deming Management Method.* New York: Dodd, Mead and Company, 1986.

Walton, Richard E., and Paul R. Lawrence. *Human Resources Management: Trends and Challenges.* Cambridge, Mass.: Harvard Business School Press, 1985.

Williams, Frederick. *Reasoning with Statistics.* New York: Holt, Reinhart, and Winston, 1986.

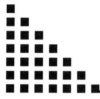

# INDEX

**Printed on Recycled Paper**